Frank Gehry's LOYOLA LAW SCHOOL

Frank Gehry's LOYOLA LAW SCHOOL

by **Robert Benson** EMERITUS PROFESSOR OF LAW

AN ARCHITECTURAL TOUR

Library of Congress Control Number 2010909985

ISBN: 978-0-615-38048-3

Loyola Law School

Loyola Marymount University, Los Angeles

PHOTO CREDITS

John Drooyan Cover, pp. 12–13, 30, 31, 32, 33, 34, 35, 45, 46–47, 55, 56, 57, 58, 62–63. John Drooyan has been photographing professionally for thirty-two years. He graduated from Loyola Law School in 2005, and practices law in San Pedro, California even as he continues his photography.

Loyola Law School archives pp. 15, 16, 17, 26–27, 28, 40–41, 43, 48, 50 **[John Skalicky]**, 51, 52, 54, 60.

Brian Costello, Loyola Law School pp. 37, 59, 70–71

Gehry Partners, LLP pp. 19, 22–23, 53, 65

Dwight Hahn, Loyola Law School Map, page 39

Design by Meryl Pollen, Los Angeles.
Printed by Typecraft Wood & Jones, Pasadena, California,
a Forest Stewardship Council certified printer.
Stock: Printed on Sterling Dull.

Contents

for Lesley Ann — *who understood*

*I suppose he'll go
down in history as the
best architect ever.*
— Penny Winton

Foreword

by **Mildred Friedman**
AUTHOR / EDITOR
The Architecture of Frank Gehry
Gehry Talks
and
Frank Gehry: The Houses

In 1978, Frank Gehry was one of twelve architects asked to submit a master plan and program for Loyola Law School, a request that would be the impetus for Gehry's objects in a landscape works to grow from domestic to public scale. It is significant to remember that 1978 was also the year that Gehry first remodeled his own Santa Monica house, exploring many of the extraordinary materials and forms that would bring the architect international renown. However, Loyola does not directly reference Gehry's house. Due to budget constraints it is less expansive in its choice of materials, and in interviews at that time, Gehry unpretentiously called himself "the cheapskate architect."

In its earliest design phase, Loyola's offices and classrooms were located in the four-story Burns Building. The Chapel and lecture halls are each in separate one-room buildings, for Gehry believes that a one-room building is as close as architecture comes to the painter facing a white canvas, a situation he often envies. Thus he proposed a village of small buildings dispersed around a plaza, and bordered by multi-purpose buildings on the campus outline. Like the Acropolis, his proposal became a pile-up of buildings, in part because its legalist clients asked for references to ancient traditions. Loyola became Gehry's only overtly historicist project, although its detached elemental columns refer to, but do not copy, classical architecture. He disdained the obvious use of historical references then used by post-modernists. Instead "he looks for awkward connections, like a jazz player just off the note." Loyola remains his only work with explicit historical motifs, and these were done at the behest of many of Loyola's more conservative faculty members. Still, Gehry's plan was controversial, and some of the most old-line members of the faculty were

vociferous in their criticisms. But as the project progressed, so did Gehry's practice, and accolades came from The New York Times and in 1989 Gehry received the coveted Pritzker Prize, and the renowned critic Paul Goldberger called the school "a triumph in the art of place making."

When Gehry opened his own office in 1962 he had shared its Venice Beach space with Chuck Arnoldi, an artist who became a life-long friend. He introduced Gehry to a number of artists whose works became significant influences on his architecture and who often became his collaborators: Claes Oldenburg, Larry Bell, Robert Rauschenberg, and Ed Ruscha among others. All of these important friendships gave Gehry's work an "edgy" quality. Oldenburg and his wife, Coosje vanBruggen, created the sculpture Toppling Ladder with Spilling Paint, which enlivens Loyola's central plaza area. Gehry also found sympathetic colleagues among younger architects. At Loyola, he brought the Frenchman Jean Nouvel in to design Minyard Tower, a glass and stainless steel structure that is attached to the Girardi building, a 2002 late addition to the campus.

It is important to be aware of Gehry's use of recurring themes in his work. The village compounds that distinguish Loyola also occur in the Benson House, the Indiana Avenue houses, the Smith House, and the Winton Guest House. Another recurring theme is the unique stairway that emerges from the Burns Academic Center. It is an expanding rectilinear passage open to the sky. This example was undoubtedly in Gehry's memory when in 2009 he began the design of a new Guggenheim Museum in Abu Dhabi. There he recalls Loyola's stairway in his proposal to use a number of cone-shaped walkways that will bring visitors in and out of the museum's central buildings.

The historic allusions at Loyola are unique in Gehry's work. With those elements subtly inserted in his singular manner, it was possible to evoke the architectural past without resorting to literal quotation. Again one finds the one-room building as a major statement in his work, a statement that comes together with his consistent use of local materials: stucco, brick, raw plywood, painted wood, metallic auto paints, and more. Together with his choice of materials, the village concept has been a consistent aspect of Gehry's mature work, and that characteristic continues to play an important role in many of his ongoing works. For Gehry never stops inventing, as he believes that "you can learn from the past but you can't continue to be in the past."

Robert Benson's careful analysis of Loyola's plan could only have been written by the faculty member most involved with the School's design since its beginning. Follow him, as he takes you on the grand tour.

Mildred Friedman NEW YORK CITY

Zig-zag stairs of **Burns Building** reflected in Chapel

Loyola Law School Meets
Frank Gehry

When St. Vincent's College of Law in Los Angeles—later renamed Loyola—admitted its first class in 1920, it was one of several new law schools across the nation intent on opening the doors of the legal profession to excluded groups. That was an era when Catholics, Jews, blacks and other minorities, as well as women, were denied entry to many law schools. The American Bar Association was crusading to keep immigrants from practicing law on the grounds that they lacked the requisite moral character of the traditional bar. At St.Vincent's, tuition was $90 a year and classes were held at night to

St. Vincent's College

Grand Avenue

allow the working class to attend. A woman was in that first class. The first African-American followed several years later. There were more than a few Irish Catholics.

The law school was part of St. Vincent's College, located in a Gothic castle designed by Albert C. Martin, a noted architect who for a half-century built numerous Los Angeles structures for the Catholic Church in historical revival styles. The 1918 building, on Venice Boulevard four miles southwest of the city center, today is the home of Loyola High School.

In the 1930s, the law school moved to the city core downtown to be nearer the courts for the convenience of faculty and students. They had found the trolly ride to Venice Boulevard an annoyance. The Jesuit fathers changed the name to Loyola Law School, opened a day division, and moved into a Spanish mission style building on Grand Avenue, which would symbolize the school for three decades.

Enrollment boomed as Loyola alumni assumed influential positions in bench and bar. By the 1960s, the Grand Avenue building could no longer hold the enrollment or the library books, so the school left downtown for a neighborhood dominated by Catholic institutions two miles west on 9th Street (now called James Wood Street), just off Olympic Boulevard at Albany Street.

The old Albert C. Martin architectural firm that had designed the Gothic castle on Venice Boulevard was brought in to build the new home of Loyola Law School: a gray-and-white stucco, two-story modernist box with a flat roof and fixed window fins. It occupied about a quarter of the square city block bounded by 9th Street, Albany Street, Olympic Boulevard and Valencia Street.

Within little more than a decade, however, enrollment had more than quadrupled. Books continued their relentless push for space in what was now one of the largest law libraries in the country. By 1978, a new building was needed. And that is when Loyola Law School met Frank Gehry.

Enter
Frank O. Gehry

Frank Gehry spent his boyhood in Toronto, where he was born as Frank Goldberg in 1929. He has often recounted his strong memories of playing in his grandfather's hardware store, of building make-believe cities from scraps of wood that his grandmother would bring home for their wood stove, and of watching the carp that she would put in the bathtub weekly before turning it into gefilte fish. Some of his architecture seems rooted, in part, in those memories.

The family moved to Los Angeles in 1947 and lived for a while in an apartment just a few blocks from where his Loyola campus stands today. He

studied architecture at the University of Southern California and urban design at Harvard, then worked for large Los Angeles architectural firms, doing shopping centers, housing and other conventional buildings.

He continued conventional work after he opened his own office in 1962, and while he took some commissions in other parts of the country, he continued as a Southern California architect who was unknown nationally. But a creative edginess began to show up in some of the projects that would eventually catapult him onto the national and international stage. He attributes the change to the yeasty group of Los Angeles and New York artists he was hanging out with in the 1960s and 70s and many of whom are still close to him today, artists like Ed Moses, Billy Al Bengston, Kenny Price, Larry Bell, Chuck Arnoldi, Ed Ruscha, Ron Davis, Robert Rauschenberg, Richard Serra, Claes Oldenburg and Coosje vanBruggen, among many others: "The way these artists thought and approached making things was a lot more intuitive and in touch with who they were. It seemed that was the way to find your voice, not the way I had been doing it. So I started mimicking their process, which was hard to do in architecture." He also mimicked their pastiche of cheap, raw industrial materials as full of aesthetic potential, most spectacularly in his own house in Santa Monica where he used corrugated metal, chain link, exposed wood lath, plywood and asphalt to transform an existing two-story bungalow into what The New York Times called a "daring," "startling" and "most significant house in Southern California in years." His national reputation was launched. That was 1978, the year Loyola Law School invited him and a dozen other Los Angeles architects to submit proposals for expansion of its campus.

Loyola Picks The Most Radical Architect

I have pondered many times the miracle that a Catholic law school with somewhat conservative, mainstream tastes picked the most radical architect available to design its new campus. How did it happen?

Of the dozen firms invited to submit proposals, seven came to the interview stage. The giant, old A.C. Martin firm that had done two of our campuses was in, along with another well-known corporate mega-firm and three moderate-sized firms respected for their quietly tasteful medium-sized buildings and fine homes. Then there were Charles Moore and Frank

Gehry. I had submitted their names to the committee after calling architecture critics and researching architectural awards. A life-long architecture buff, I had immediately volunteered to be on the architectural selection committee, sensing that this could be an opportunity for Loyola to leave a legacy that extended beyond the world of law.

Moore, the congenial dean of the architecture school at UCLA, was known nationally for flamboyant works, including the Sea Ranch condominiums on California's Sonoma coast and Kresge College at the Santa Cruz campus of the University of California. His name was brought up by all the critics I talked to, as was Frank Gehry's. With Gehry, though, words like "hot," "eccentric," "experimental," and "avant garde" were let loose. When I mentioned Gehry's name to the architectural consultant our committee had hired to help us, he said, "Now you're talking architecture with a capital A."

At the interviews, our committee did not see a hot eccentric in Frank Gehry. Presentations by the big corporate firms had been slick and patronizing. The medium-sized firms seemed to want to repeat their past projects and lacked confidence to think of something new for us. Charles Moore was amusing and fresh. Frank Gehry was just his unpretentious, down-to-earth self.

The others gave us glossy graphics. Gehry took masking tape and posted up a roll of brown wrapping paper around the conference room, a black marker displaying his ideas and timeline. That, and the fact that he called himself "the cheapskate architect," appealed to the Catholic tradition of respect for poverty, not to mention our budget.

He showed slides of his recent mainstream work: the Rouse Company headquarters in Columbia, Maryland; the UCLA Placement Center; a Westinghouse distribution center in an industrial park; the interior of a small Los Angeles law firm; an outdoor concert pavilion in Concord, California. He had with him two buttoned-down partners who seemed as conventional as city managers. The projects in the slides did exhibit unusual creativity and bits of odd materials like plywood and chain-link, but I don't recall a focus on his truly eccentric ideas—at least until he flashed a slide on the screen of an elephant standing on top of his cardboard furniture. It looked like a circus trick. My colleagues shot furtive glances at one another. I thought, "Uh-oh, he's going over the top here—they're going to think he's nuts." After he left, someone on the committee said, "What in the world does an elephant have to do with a law school?" I think it was at that point that Dean Fred Lower, chair of the committee and a fellow with conservative tastes who I feared would be unenthusiastic about Gehry, remarked, "This guy is the closest thing to an original thinker I've ever met. I like that."

Gehry's early sketch of a village of buildings around a plaza

And Gehry had a huge original idea for Loyola. All the other architects had proposed a single, massive building to accommodate our space needs. Gehry proposed a village of smaller buildings around a plaza. It would, he said, give us a sense of place, on a human scale. The idea captivated the committee. That idea, plus the promise of a low-cost budget and the fact that Gehry didn't talk down to us, won the competition for him.

The committee was composed of seven members: Dean Fred Lower, professors Chris May, Don Wilson and myself, Librarian Frederica Sedgwick, Loyola Marymount University vice president John Pfaffinger, and consultant Richard Hutman. Gehry had six first place votes and one second. I may have been the only one to rank him first on the basis that he was a cutting-edge radical. The others, mostly a group of cautious moderates, put him first because of his village concept, his projected budget, and his modest demeanor.

There were other hurdles to overcome before Gehry became, and stayed, campus architect. The Board of Trustees of the University had final approval, and the word came back that they were not eager for Gehry. I shot off a strong memo to faculty and trustees arguing that the trustees owed deference to the law school committee that had clearly done its homework. There were discussions behind the scenes. In the end, the trustees signed off on our selection.

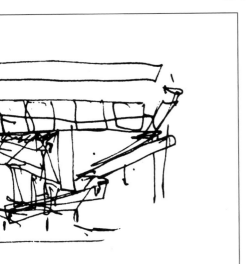

By 1981, when the first three of Loyola's buildings were being completed, Gehry's reputation for radicalism had spread so much that he felt compelled to deliver a talk to an architectural conference entitled, "I Am Not Weird." At Loyola, the new campus was controversial. Students and faculty were shocked by the bright yellow color of the Burns Building, quibbled about the zigzag outside metal staircases, wondered when the plywood ceilings and duct work would be covered up inside, complained about acoustics, and accused the freestanding stucco columns of being wasted money. A faculty blowhard sent around a memo suggesting we hire a foreign air force to bomb it and start over. Once again, the trustees and administration were restless. Rumors circulated that they wanted someone less controversial than Gehry to finish the campus plan. I wrote another memo that rankled the trustees and the administration, accompanied by my unquiet resignation from the construction oversight committee.

Then the accolades began coming in. First the architectural magazines here and abroad, next the local press, then The New York Times and Time Magazine. The Getty Museum began sending bus tours of museum directors down for a visit, and travel agencies from Japan and Australia put the campus on their itineraries for Los Angeles. There was also the PBS TV special on American architecture comparing Loyola to Thomas Jefferson's design for the University of Virginia. The publicity impressed Loyola's doubters. Gehry was retained to complete the planned construction. Eventually, some of those who had favored dismissing him were boasting of having hired him in the first place.

Loyola's campus was Frank Gehry's first major project to draw national and international attention. In 1989, he was awarded the international Pritzker Prize, architecture's most prestigious honor. The award cited the Loyola campus, among other works, as the basis of the prize. In 1997, he stunned the design world with his Guggenheim Museum in Bilbao, Spain, and in 2003 did so again with the Disney Concert Hall in Los Angeles.

In 2002, United States Supreme Court Justice Anthony Kennedy dedicated the Girardi Advocacy Center at Loyola, marking more than 20 years of Gehry-designed work for the law school campus. In 2009, the lead by the architecture critic for the Los Angeles Times marking Gehry's 80th birthday read: "Frank Gehry, who turned 80 on Saturday, is the most famous architect in the world by a healthy margin."

Architectural Overview
of the Campus

<u>A Sense of Place</u> The Loyola campus catches you by surprise. It is possible to miss it altogether as you drive by and see only the rather blank face the school offers to the neighborhood. But once inside, you emerge into a space that Paul Goldberger, architecture critic for The New York Times, called "a triumph in the art of place-making."

Gehry was derided as the "bad boy" of architecture, principally because of his use of cheap industrial materials like chain-link, sheet-metal, plywood, and asphalt, partly because of his radical forms and designs, like the one for a house whose rooms, including a hallway, were unconnected, free-standing pieces. What others saw as crazy ideas, Gehry saw as imaginative use of the materials and culture of late 20th century Los Angeles. By the late 1980s much of the world had come to see it his way. Today both the avant garde and the establishment embrace him as the international leader of architectural creativity.

When he was still hotly controversial, Loyola selected him from among a dozen contenders to expand the Law School. When we told him we just needed one big building, he nudged, "What would you think of a campus?"

And that was his first gift to Loyola: Between 1981 and 1991, he transformed this small city block on the margins of downtown L.A. to "recapture the sense of a special place," as it was put in a PBS television documentary on American architecture, which compared Frank Gehry's design for Loyola to Thomas Jefferson's "academical village" at the University of Virginia. Even if you are normally oblivious to your physical environment, walking into Loyola you will be hit with the sensation that you have arrived someplace indeed. You may think that you have wandered onto a surreal stage set for an ancient Mediterranean town.

A place for people

Before the 1980s, the School consisted of one crowded, modernist box containing classroooms, administrative and faculty offices (now remodeled to house the Rains Library), the ultra-functionalist parking structure, and a few trailer-classrooms. That was it. There was no here here. Students and faculty could not wait to get out, zooming from car to classroom and home again.

Now it is hard to catch this campus when it is not peopled with characters—students, faculty, staff, visitors—sitting, talking, lizarding, reading, eating, studying, playing, or on the move around the miniature "academical village," enjoying the place as a place.

Columns outside **Merrifield Hall**

<u>A Sense of History</u>   The month that he was given the go-ahead for Loyola, Gehry had scheduled a trip to Greece and Rome. There he was, ambling through the Acropolis and the Forum with sketchbook in hand, recalling that many of the Loyola faculty had urged him to recreate symbols from the law's past in Plato and Cicero, Coke and Blackstone, Jefferson and the American neoclassical courthouse tradition. Gehry disdained the facile use of historical references that post-modern architects were making their hallmark. Loyola is his only work with explicit historical motifs, but he did it at the behest of the lawyers.

When he returned, his sketchbook was inked with thin, squiggly images for Loyola: columns, pediments, and colonnades amidst not one but a bunch of buildings, grouped around a town-like space as in the Acropolis or the Forum. He made no effort, however, to reconstruct a literal, historic Greek or Roman setting, the way Hollywood or a mall developer would do. With suggestive, minimal forms, he evoked the feel of the ancient decayed sites as they are today. When you walk by the stucco columns outside Merrifield Hall and the Hall of the '70s, you sense a bit of the bulk, the roundness, the height, the shadows of columns you may brush by in the ruins of Rome or Athens.

There is the outline of a Babylonian ziggurat in the cinderblocks covering the Olympic Boulevard exit from Donovan Hall. There is a Romanesque chapel, replete with bell tower, sunken a few steps down from the plaza, the way old churches in Venice or Bologna or Florence are often sinking from centuries of subsidence. Coming into Merrifield Hall, there is a ramp that echoes the ones running up Egyptian pyramids. A ramp was required for wheelchair access, but instead of sneaking it unobtrusively in a side door, Gehry made it the main processional entrance. The oak tree in the center of the plaza sits atop what could have been a pyramid washed down over the centuries.

<u>A Sense of Chaos</u>   The historical allusions by themselves are enough to suggest a dizzying complexity. There is, however, much more, and it adds up to a deliberate theme of post-modern chaos running through the architecture.

Frank Gehry declines to put himself in any school of architectural thought, and rejects the label "post-modernist" which in architecture has come to mean buildings that incorporate historical references. Loyola is the sole Gehry project with explicit historical references, and those were in response to the law professors urging them, so the term in that sense does not fit him well. But the term post-modern is also used broadly in cultural history to refer to a profound change that has occurred in virtually every practical and intellectual field, including architecture, following modernism. Life is different at

the end of the twentieth and beginning of the twenty-first century. The post-modern approach has to do with deconstructing things and reassembling them like collages from different points of view. Today's architects, at least the creative ones, feel that their challenge is to throw off the stylistic shackles of their modernist predecessors, just as the modernists threw off the shackles of their predecessors. It is fair to call them post-modernists, with or without historical references. They are into "smashing the modernist box," going for inconsistent richness of meaning rather than clarity of meaning, celebrating "messy vitality" rather than modernist rationalism. In this, no one surpasses Frank Gehry.

Loyola Law School actually offers a restrained example of Gehry's potential for creative chaos. His most dramatic act is to crash the great central stairway and glass atrium into the modernist box of the Burns Building at several sharp, zigzagging angles, and to echo that with wild metal zigzag stairways at either end.

Central stairway and atrium of **Burns Building**

More subtly, he takes you up the first flight of the green central stairs at an angle, with your feet facing the Burns facade straight-on while your body is jostled to the right by the handrails, all in a flight of steps which narrows rapidly in order to fool the eye into seeing greater depth through the old Renaissance perspective trick of running parallel lines together. More subtly yet, he has put the central stairway slightly off-center, mullioned the windows in an asymmetrical pattern, and put a playful false window cut-out on the third-story stairway landing.

Then there is the powerful metal sculpture that juts like a castle gate from the vertical box of the Casassa Building, hovering over a delicate glass jewel box of a skylight. There is the hole in the Donovan Hall skylight, which permits rain to sheet down the glass right above the professor's lectern. There is the bell tower with no bell, and the reversal of the altar in the chapel so that worshipers have to enter and turn around to face the priest (which caused a momentary theological contretemps). All these were deliberate irrationalities.

The smorgasbord of incongruous materials adds to the contradictions and complexity. There is copper cladding on the chapel and the square columns outside Merrifield. There is stucco, some a natural grey hue, some orange, some a dazzling ochre, some terra-cotta. There is 20th century sheet metal wrapping the ancient forms of columns. There is brick, and glass and concrete. There is plywood. No chain link. (Loyola vetoed it.)

A Sense of Beauty   Yet, for all of its radical mix of history, crude and polished materials, startling shapes and irrationalities, the architecture exudes an overall magisterial, original beauty. A poignant place to see this is in the interior of the chapel, but the beauty is exhibited as well in the larger composition of the campus as a whole. "[Gehry] has virtually invented a new form of late-20th century urban classicism, simultaneously gritty and dignified," Time Magazine has written of Loyola's campus. This is the genius that sets

Frank Gehry apart, the reason that in any given week you are likely to spot art and architecture students from Los Angeles and indeed from throughout the world prowling the campus with pencils or cameras trying to figure out Gehry's formula. There is no formula. Each project is a fresh composition of sculptures that corresponds, individually and as a group, to the extraordinary visions that float into Gehry's head.

Each of the buildings is a separate sculpture, each an original form that had never before emerged in architectural consciousness. True, there are the historical allusions already mentioned, but where had anyone ever before seen shapes like the metal and glass affair protruding from the facade of the Casassa building, or the great tall sheet metal columns rising through the entrance wall of Donovan, or the dark green central stairway of Burns snaking sideways when seen from the plaza in front of the cafeteria?

And the individual sculptures connect to form a whole. The tall Casassa talks to the the tall Donovan across the plaza. Merrifield's angles link visually to the angles of the chapel and the Burns central stair. The terra-cotta Girardi building joins Donovan, Burns, Merrifield and Casassa like a set of colored children's blocks. The vertical spire of the Minyard Tower appended

Towers of **Chapel, Donovan** and **Girardi**

left profile of **Burns** central stairway

to Girardi joins the vertical spires of the columns on Donovan and the chapel's bell tower. There are numerous other visual threads that weave the pieces together and produce the feeling that, for all its discord, there is an overall harmony to this composition—for all its grit, there is dignity.

Finding Your Own Niche   If you are destined to spend some years on this campus you will begin to read the architecture in your own way and make it your own, discovering the daily pleasures of the niches of beauty hidden here. For starters, try some of these: Laugh at the way these blocky buildings are alive with motion: the metal gate plunging from Casassa, the central and end stairways jutting from Burns' facade, the "Toppling Ladder" sculpture by Oldenburg and van Bruggen egging them on. Gehry later became renowned as the man who could make buildings seem literally to dance, but he was doing it here early on. Then, liberate yourself from ground level by going to the top of the glass-and-mirror-metal Minyard Tower attached to Girardi, designed by famed French architect Jean Nouvel at Gehry's invitation. From there, check out the city skyline and campus views framed by slices of glass as you descend level by level.

Sit in the well of the chapel bell tower, reading a book and spying on the rest of the campus from below ground level. Smell the wood in the chapel. Take a front row seat in Donovan in order to look at the sky overhead while the professor is talking. Tease your sense of vertigo and history by sitting in the Hall of the '80s, which is reminiscent of steep amphitheater medical classrooms of medieval universities. Study the line of the west handrail and birch plywood light sculptures in the Hall of the 80s, and run your fingers over the plywood walls on the way out. Feel the plywood sandwiches of the study desks in the Darling Library Pavilion, then walk down the Darling stairs to catch the view through the glass jewel box skylight. Climb the central stairway of Burns looking straight up at the complex sculptures above your head. Toss pennies from the balcony of the Burns' central stair onto the tops of the Merrifield columns. Walk down the third-floor corridor of Burns to see natural light piercing two stories into the building. Arrive at the south patio on top of Burns just in time to see the sun setting behind the palms in the western sky, but first look northeast to see it putting the orange facade of Casassa ablaze.

After your last class some night, take a walk down the dizzying metal staircase off the north patio of Burns' roof, but wait until a night when, there among the shimmering downtown skyscrapers, a full moon floats.

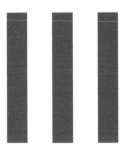

A Walking Tour

<u>Oak tree quad and Oldenburg/vanBruggen sculpture</u> Let's begin our walking tour by sitting down—on the steps under the big oak tree in the central plaza. The plaza has the relaxed and sunny feel of plazas you may have enjoyed in Italy, France, Spain. And, as is often the case in European plazas, important buildings line the perimeter: the great halls of teaching in Merrifield, Donovan and Girardi; the offices of the professors, administrators and student

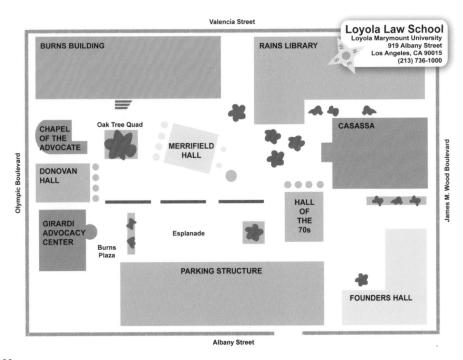

oak tree quad and sculpture in front of **Merrifield Hall**

organizations, as well as small classrooms in Burns; the chapel; and, of course, Sonia's cafeteria, whose food and drink you may carry to the movable tables with umbrellas dotting the plaza.

The columns in front of Merrifield and the steps around the oak tree provide a classic backdrop for speaking to a public audience. Gehry was quoted in 1985 in the Loyola Law Review: "I always envisioned somebody standing in the middle—between those columns—and spontaneously spouting forth great ideas. You lawyers talk so well. I hope it is used that way. I hope you do that." We do do that sometimes.

Near the oak at the center of the plaza is the sculpture by Claes Oldenburg and Coosje vanBruggen, "Toppling Ladder with Spilling Paint." Oldenburg, one of the legendary fathers of the Pop Art movement, and his collaborator and late wife, vanBruggen, are internationally acclaimed for superscaled renditions of commonplace objects in public places: the baseball bat in Chicago, the clothespin in Philadelphia, the flashlight in Las Vegas, the cherry on a spoon in Minneapolis, the toothbrush in Germany, the saw in Tokyo, and many others.

Among the closest of Gehry's many long-time artist friends, the sculptors visited Loyola shortly after the first buildings were up, and Gehry showed them the spot where the sculpture stands today. It's about ten feet from the last of the four stucco columns standing outside Merrifield. Gehry mentioned that he had designed a fifth column, lying on the ground, to go there. It was to be a reference to historical ruins as in Rome and Athens, adding movement to the stationary columns and resonating with the movement of the green central staircase of Burns close behind. It was a little crazy for ordinary folks, and Loyola vetoed it, as Loyola had vetoed chain-link.

A couple years later, "Toppling Ladder with Spilling Paint" was unveiled, an outsized ladder made partially of chain-link, caught at the moment of falling over and spilling a can of blue paint off its top. The artists had found a way to add the missing kinetic energy to the spot, and add chain-link, in an homage to Gehry. Funded by a grant from the Times-Mirror Foundation, the sculpture was dedicated in September of 1986 in an evening ceremony that drew much of the Los Angeles art community.

Hanging out with students and staff in the plaza that week, Oldenburg and vanBruggen were asked what it meant. VanBruggen offered the metaphor of the scales of justice, except that instead of being made of gold and in ideal balance, the real-world scales of justice are made of everyday stuff and are falling over. Oldenburg accepted every meaning thrown at him by students and staff, finally agreeing that it is best seen as a contrivance to generate interpretations. It seems safe to say that it may be a cynical comment on the law and it is certainly humorous. But maybe not. After the artists and the crowd had departed, I noticed a library staff friend sitting on the oak tree steps, staring at the sculpture. I came and sat next him. "So, what do you think?" I asked. He looked up, eyes brimming with tears. "You have no idea what they've done here," he said softly.

Fritz B. Burns Building   The law school's largest building, Burns is a bright yellow four-story box split in two by a dark green central staircase that snakes its way to the top and ends in a glass atrium with a classical pediment. Through the glass you catch vivid colors of a mural in the atrium.

Two other staircases descend the facade on either end. Gehry was quoted about them in the Loyola Law Review at the time: "I took the stairways that would normally have been inside and spilled them onto the outside of the building with the idea that it would animate the facade and bring people out onto the front of the building, animating the building with human beings. That does work. When classes break, you see the front of the building covered with people running up and down the stairs. That complements the people walking around in the space below and gives it a lot more excitement. Keeping the stairs on the outside was cheaper than putting them inside because it was more like a fire escape. You weren't buying the enclosure of so much space."

Note the asymmetries in the facade: the Baroque central staircase is off-center, window mullions are inconsistent, a window with no glass appears on the third-floor landing. This is a modernist box deconstructed.

Along the colonnade on the ground floor is a series of small offices for student organizations, like street-level shops in a village, facing out through glass doors and windows. Unfortunately, successive inhabitants have defeated the architectural gift by covering the glass with blinds and posters. This is also true of the staff office next to the cafeteria, whose generous glass windows and doors are usually darkened like a cave, impeding human contact for those inside and out. Sonia's Cafeteria anchors the north corner, and its expansive windows do promote human contact and merge inside and outside. Sonia's is named for the late Sonia de Sotelo, a Panamanian cafeteria worker whose smile and ringing voice lifted the spirits of customers for years.

Inside Take the elevator to the top atrium. Aside from dazzling views of the campus and the downtown cityscape, here you get close to "The Fall of Icarus" by noted Los Angeles muralist Kent Twitchell, based on a collage by artist Jim Morphesis, both commissioned with grants from Times-Mirror Foundation. Gehry had indicated the spot for a colorful mural, but the artists were selected by a competition held by Loyola.

Exit the atrium either north or south and walk along the narrow corridor, half of which is taken by a running skylight shaft that brings sun to the third floor below. Note the pale jade green paint that is one of Gehry's favorite colors. This is a quiet, somewhat monastic floor, with only professors' offices. At the end of the corridor, walk outside and get a small thrill descending the open metal stairway to the third floor.

The third floor is packed with offices of professors and secretaries, more than Gehry designed. It has lost its original spaciousness as the school keeps subdividing it. Walk the length of the corridor and descend the metal stairway to the second floor.

Gehry once referred to the second floor as the "piano nobile," Italian for the large apartments occupied by the nobility above the street level shops in Renaissance buildings. The nobles here are the deans and administrators. Gehry designed a simple, elegant suite of offices for them, but the space has unfortunately been subdivided with cubicles and walls. There are also an information desk, a few professors' offices, and three small classrooms. The classrooms look out at the stage-set of the campus through enormous windows—or they would if instructors and students would ever raise the blinds.

Walk to the information desk in the center, then out and down the last flight of the green central staircase, onto the plaza. Circle back into the inside ground level of the building to check out the student lounge, with its exposed ducting, uplighting, and clerestory windows.

<u>Father Donald P. Merrifield Hall</u> Other buildings play with historical fragments, but Merrifield actually looks like a Greek temple, or an early American courthouse in the classical revival style.

Notice that it sits in the plaza at an angle. One of the trustees noticed this too while reviewing the model at Gehry's office in 1980. He remarked, "Oh this has been knocked crooked," and straightened the little wooden Merrifield piece on the grid. Gehry skewed it back, saying, "No, it's supposed to be that way." A disagreement ensued. Gehry, steaming, called me and complained the trustees were interfering. He told me, "I'm right about this. You'll see and feel the volume of the building much more if you come at it from an angle. The Greeks knew this. Look at the Parthenon. When you approach it on the Acropolis, it's from an angle." I endeared myself with the trustees by accusing them of meddling with artistic genius. But the word came down: Merrifield would sit straight in the plaza.

Father Donald P. Merrifield Hall north entrance

Merrifield interior

The day the backhoe dug the trenches for Merrifield's foundation, I called Gehry, excited: "Frank! I'm watching the backhoe dig the trenches and it's going in at your original skewed angle!" "Oh," he said, "I thought I lost that battle. I guess somebody forgot to change the blueprints."

On the east wall you see three large indented panels of grey stucco. They seem to beckon murals. On the model, Gehry had pasted colorful magazine reproductions of nineteenth century paintings of George Washington and other founding fathers, this after professors urged him to recognize the law and the Constitution in the architecture. I thought the model was a kitsch joke, but many of the faculty thought it was the right stuff.

We had formed an art committee to acquire original art from emerging Los Angeles artists for some of the interior spaces, and the committee undertook to find an artist and raise funds for the Merrifield murals. We agreed, though, that Frank Gehry would have the final word because the murals were an integral part of his architecture. We could not find an artist he was enthusiastic about, and after a long while he came to us with a proposal from his friend Ed Ruscha. Ruscha was, and is, an internationally renowned conceptual artist. He had mocked up on the model of Merrifield three black slate panels with four words engraved in white, each diminishing in size. First panel: "What." Second panel: "is." Third panel: "the law?" It could be seen as profound. It could be seen as ironic.

Ruscha, Gehry, our art consultant Ellie Blankfort, and I carried the model into then-Dean Arthur Frakt's office to get his approval. Frakt had been quite supportive of the art program, but before even being introduced to Ruscha, he shot a look at the model and declared, "Oh, no you don't!", then proceeded to make sharp remarks about his responsibility to alumni and trustees. In short, he didn't care for it. Ruscha walked out without saying a word, followed by the rest of us. Years went by. Gehry told me once that he had grown to like the blank panels. Another ironic irrationality in the architecture?

Inside, Merrifield is a theater-style classroom seating 125 students. There were problems with acoustics early on, which were finally resolved by placing a swarm of beautiful flying plywood wedges overhead. Gehry's raw construction look is at full expression in the ceiling. The desktops are not Gehry's original color.

<u>Chapel of the Advocate</u>   The chapel is like a cartoon sketch of a tiny Romanesque church preserved behind museum glass. Mass is celebrated here four times a week. The tower and chapel sit below plaza level, as if from ancient subsidence of the earth. They were originally covered with a plywood

from Finland that had the color of polished mahogany, an experimental material for Gehry that didn't weather well, so he replaced it with copper. Looking through the glass, you don't see the altar and seats but see a wall, painted Gehry's favored pale jade green, that houses the priest's accoutrements. You must enter to see the full space, and when you do you first smell the wood and then see sheets of pristine plywood and unfinished joists arranged with simple beauty. It proves that the raw construction look can be truly elegant.

Note that you enter and turn around to sit facing the altar. This is contrary to Catholic tradition and was the subject of intense discussions, but in the end won acceptance after Gehry said he saw sitting in the curved apse as sitting in the cupped hand of God. The colorful Garden of Eden stained glass window, donated by Professor Michael Josephson, is by noted Los Angeles artist Michael Todd. It was chosen in a competition held by the art committee. Gehry was not happy with the way it changed the feel of the chapel.

Father Joseph Donovan Hall The historical precedent for the form of Donovan Hall is misty, though it bears some resemblance to a profile of Michelangelo's gateway to Rome called the Porta Pia. In any event, the stately columns shoot-

Donovan Hall at night

ing high up the front seem to make some strong comment about history. On the model, Gehry had put a small Byzantine gold dome, but that was later deleted, apparently for reasons of cost. Inside is another large theater classroom, with 98 seats, but the short depth of the room makes it seem almost intimate. The desktops are not Gehry's original color. The raw construction ceiling is again on display. Over the lectern where the professor stands rises the tall skylight box. Remarkably, it is actually open to the sky down to the glass over the lectern. Raindrops land just above the lecturer's head.

Albert H. Girardi Advocacy Center   The three-story Girardi is a late addition, built in 2002 after Gehry's style had changed dramatically to the computer-enabled, voluptuous forms of the Bilbao Guggenheim and the Los Angeles Disney. Here he chose to stay with his earlier style of breaking and rearranging boxy forms. Girardi is just a box. No historical references. No asymmetries. But it is a strikingly beautiful box, a rich terra-cotta that joins the yellow of Burns and the orange of Casassa like a set of children's colored blocks.

The box is deconstructed considerably by the Minyard Tower appended to it like a giant tube of lipstick. French architect Jean Nouvel, later another

Albert H. Girardi Advocacy Center

Pritzker Prize winner, did the tower at Gehry's invitation. In its polished stainless steel you catch endless mirrored fragments of surrounding buildings. The swirling angles of the stainless steel were to relate to an adjacent auditorium proposed by Gehry but never built.

Enter the building and take the elevator to the top, exiting, then opening the door to the tower. You realize now that the tower can't be used to climb or descend the building because its landings don't connect vertically. Each is a self-contained viewing platform, just for fun. The glass is so clear that it seems open and gives you vertigo. You feel the architecture, as you do on the Eiffel Tower or on the zigzag staircases of the Burns Building. Views of the campus and the city skyline are framed in discrete slices. Here you get a good view of the elementary school across Albany Street, whose architects made their school remarkably sensitive to Loyola's style and scale. Repeat the experience landing by landing, until you reach the ground floor.

The ground floor is devoted entirely to the high-tech Robinson courtroom, the pièce de resistance of Loyola's teaching rooms. Large lecture classes are given here but it is principally for moot court presentations in which students play advocacy roles before panels of judges. Sometimes there is nothing moot about it: California and federal courts occasionally hold full sessions here, moving lawyers and judges to Loyola for the day.

Gehry's raw construction style has given way here to a more refined veneer of rich color, but the wood is nevertheless plywood. Always letting light and the outside in, he has placed a large window in the north wall, once again an architectural gift that is too often overlooked by inhabitants indifferent to a blind pulled down when there is no need. There is a gem of a jury room hidden in the southeast corner.

The second floor is occupied by the "Courtroom of the '90s," a smaller version of Robinson. It is named for the alumni of the decade of the 1990s whose donations paid for it. The third floor contains a small classroom, several interview and negotiation studios, and the instructional media tech center from which sessions in most rooms on campus can be remotely recorded for student review.

Proposed auditorium   At the dedication ceremony for the Girardi building in 2002, presided over by United States Supreme Court Justice Anthony Kennedy, Gehry recounted his nearly quarter-century of development of the

model of proposed auditorium

Loyola campus, and told the audience that one last building was needed to complete the composition. The school had asked him to propose a large auditorium to replace the need to erect rented tents on the esplanade several times a year for crowds like the one assembled that day. At the same time he designed Girardi, Gehry did a model for a rather Bilbaoesque auditorium on the grassy area in front of it. Loyola has not moved forward with the proposal.

<u>Esplanade and parking structure</u> Walk north from Girardi across the esplanade until you reach the outdoor coffee stand for a pick-me-up drink. Have a seat and scan the esplanade and parking structure.

The large space of the esplanade is usually empty but is often set up with tables or tents for special events like the public interest job fair, the swearing-in of alumni newly admitted to the bar, outdoor barbecues, and so forth.

parking structure

The parking structure was completed in 1994 to replace one damaged in an earthquake. The budget dictated a sparse, utilitarian structure. In a simple move, Gehry—among other things the foremost architect of metal—saw an opportunity for a long, inexpensive sheet metal facade to hide the cement-block structure and make it look rather like a real building. Cutouts that look like windows, but aren't, run floor by floor, and they as well as the size and shape of the building turn it into a sort of colorless palimpsest of the Burns Building across the way.

Hall of the '70s From the coffee stand, which froths its lattes smack against the side of Hall of the '70s, walk around to the front where five freestanding stucco columns and a pediment announce this as another little Greek temple, like Merrifield. This one is smaller and plainer, a virtually colorless grey stucco. It is named for the alumni of the 1970s decade who contributed to fund it. Like Donovan, it has a rather intimate feel inside, making for good discussions. Purple table tops have replaced Gehry's color scheme, and the electric switch controlling blinds above the skylight over the lectern has been disconnected,

Father Charles S. Casassa Building and **Darling Pavilion**

replaced with an unopenable screen blocking the sun. It's done to keep the room always dark in case the high-tech audio-vusual equipment is used at any moment. Technology trumps nature.

<u>Father Charles S. Casassa Building</u> Casassa is the most flamboyant building on campus, with its sheet metal wedge hovering four stories in the air supported by an arm that looks like it could be on a hinge. I can't help seeing it as a castle gate about to slam down, but whatever it suggests it is a unique fantasy that had not appeared before in architecture. Wrapping into the building from the left is another sheet metal structure, an enclosed curved bridge from Rains Library supported by metal columns. Floating behind it all is the bright orange stucco box of Casassa. Together, it is an extraordinary collage.

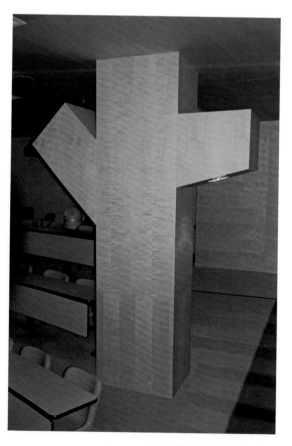

light pillar in **Hall of the '80s**

Enter Casassa at the first-floor level on the upper plaza. Walk straight down the corridor past clinical offices from which students and supervising lawyers dispense legal services to the outside community. At the end of the corridor, open the door to the Hall of the '80s (named for the alumni of that decade who funded it) and you will suddenly find yourself at the top of a 90-seat tiered gallery so steep it seems like a carnival ride. Students must resist the impulse to sail paper airplanes down to the podium. If you have been to Gehry's Disney Concert Hall, you have seen beautiful blonde plywood and light pillars that resemble flowers. The Hall of the '80s was an earlier example of both.

Walk down to the podium, then take the exit door behind it into the basement level of the building where you will see three small seminar rooms and the bookstore. Opposite the bookstore, take the elevator to the fifth floor at the top. (It will not stop at floors 2, 3, or 4 because those floors contain books accessible only from the secure Rains Library.) The fifth floor houses additional important community clinical programs and, on the south end, a small administrative office with the best view on campus. You can see the same

Casassa Building detail

view by walking into the conference room next to it, which is almost always empty. Here is the ultimate bird's-eye view of Loyola.

You will see the rest of Casassa by entering through Rains Library, so take the elevator to the first floor, go outside, and walk into Rains.

<u>William M. Rains Library</u> This is the old two-story building by the A.C. Martin firm that housed the entire school from 1965 to 1981. It now houses only books and library materials, one of the largest private law collections west of the Mississippi. When asked what to do with the building, Frank Gehry replied, "Blow it up." Instead, though, he cleared walls to make flowing space, cut a long skylight in the roof to let sunshine penetrate the central reading room, and installed his trademark tables of sandwiched plywood.

From the central reading room on the second floor, find the bridge to the Darling Pavilion, which extends the library into floors 2, 3 and 4 of the Casassa building. Essentially book stacks and study rooms, it is nevertheless

William M. Rains Library

of architectural interest. Note the attractive furniture and the exquisite, complex sculptural views from each stair landing, out through the glass box that perches under the facade's metal extravaganza.

The library displays many works of the school's significant fine art collection.

Founders Hall Our tour ends at Founders Hall. Walk behind the Hall of the '70s and look across the small quadrangle. Founders is the two-story red brick building hugging the north and east edges. For many years the headquarters of Catholic Charities, Loyola purchased it in the 1990s, thus completing the acquisition of this entire square block. The building contains several major administrative offices, plus clinics, student organizations and two seminar rooms. The remodeled spaces are pleasant, but architecturally there is little of interest inside. Outside, however, Gehry has stamped the old building with his imprimatur and tied it into the rest of the campus with a brilliant, minimalist, inexpensive addition of a tilted metal canopy.

There is one more thing to note from the front of Founders Hall. Here, you see the surprising east side of Casassa in a startling profile that makes you realize you had not yet really seen Casassa.

And that ends
our tour. Time for
another latte.

pp. 62 – 63 **Casassa Building** east side

Bibliography: Frank Gehry at Loyola

1979

Joe W. Anguiano, "Loyola Law School plans expansion," Los Angeles Times, December 16, 1979, p. VII-1.

1981

Joseph Giovannini, "Loyola receives both sides of the architectural case," Los Angeles Herald Examiner, August 24, 1981.

"Architect of the year: Frank Gehry," arts + architecture (Los Angeles, Fall 1981).

1982

John V. Mutlow, "Loyola Law School/Frank O. Gehry & Associates," L.A. Architect, January, 1982.

Joseph Morgenstern, "The Gehry style," The New York Times Magazine, May 16, 1982, p. 48.

John Dreyfuss, "AIA Awards Reveal Diversity of Design in L.A.," Los Angeles Times, October 22, 1982, p. V-1.

Global Architecture GA Document 5 (Tokyo, 1982).

The California Condition: A Pregnant Architecture (La Jolla Museum of Contemporary Art, 1982).

1983

Robert Coombs, "Post-modernism has arrived," Los Angeles Herald Examiner, March 30, 1983, p. B-1.

Lindsay Stamm Shapiro, "A minimalist architecture of allusion: current projects of Frank Gehry," Architectural Record, June 1983, p. 114.

"Most Creative Law Building," L.A. Weekly, September 29 – October 7, 1983.

1984

Roger Kempler, "Frank Gehry: Understanding the urban campus," The Loyola Reporter, March 14, 1984, p. 1.

Leon Whiteson, "Frank Gehry's buildings invent their own order," Los Angeles Herald Examiner, July 29, 1984, p. D-1.

Leon Whiteson, "An architect captures L. A. tensions in solid form," Los Angeles Herald Examiner, August 26, 1984, p. E-10.

Diana Rico, "Frank Gehry," City Magazine International (Paris, November 1984), p. 14.

Barbara Flanagan, "The Nation: Los Angeles Civic Subversion," Art News (New York, December 1984), p. 129.

1985

Mason Andrews, Frank Gehry: Buildings and Projects (Rizzoli, New York, 1985).

Global Architecture GA Document 12 (Tokyo, 1985).

Cross Currents of American Architecture (Andreas Papadakis, ed., Architectural Design AD Editions, London, 1985).

"Frank O. Gehry and Associates," 19 Architecture in Greece (Greek language) 1985.

Pilar Viladas, "Form follows ferment," Progressive Architecture (Cleveland, February, 1985), p. 67.

William Fulton, "Loyola Law School bears Gehry's mark," Evening Outlook (Santa Monica), March 29, 1985, Weekend Supplement, p. 6.

William Fulton, "Architect's playful hand seen in Loyola's new campus," Los Angeles Daily Journal, April 1, 1985, p. II-1.

John Pastier, "Loyola Law School Los Angeles," Architecture: The American Institute of Architects Journal (New York, May, 1985).

Dominique Lyon, "Frank O. Gehry: Avis de tempete sur le Pacifique," AA L'Architecture d' Aujourd"hui (Paris, June 1985), p. 85.

Robert W. Benson, "Tribute to the new architecture," 19 Loyola of Los Angeles Law Review (November, 1985 at xiii).

Frank O. Gehry, "Description of the new architecture," 19 Loyola of Los Angeles Law Review (November, 1985 at xii; December, 1985 at xiii; May, 1986 at xvii; June, 1986 at xvii).

1986

The Architecture of Frank Gehry (Walker Art Center, Minneapolis; Rizzoli, New York, 1986).

Robert A. M. Stern, Pride of Place: Building the American Dream (book accompanying PBS television series of same name) (Houghton Mifflin, Boston & New York, 1986).

Architecture and Urbanism (a + u Publishing, Tokyo, January, 1986).

Kurt Anderson, "Design: Best of '85," Time, January 6, 1986, p. 102.

Sam Hall Kaplan, "Circling in on design for a square," Los Angeles Times, May 18, 1986, p. VIII-2.

Paul Goldberger, "A Show That Gets Inside The Work of Frank Gehry," The New York Times, October 5, 1986, p. H-31.

Kurt Anderson, "Building beauty the hard way," Time, October 13, 1986, p. 108.

Martin Filler, "Mavrick Master," House & Garden (Beverly Hills & New York, November, 1986), p. 208.

1987

"Art, architecture and the law at a Los Angeles law school, Sunset Magazine, March 1987.

Paul Gapp, "A gentle maverick," Chicago Tribune, March 15, 1987, Section 13, p. 4.

Michael Webb, "A man who made architecture an art of the unexpected," Smithsonian, April, 1987, p. 48.

Benjamin Forgey, "Architecture On the Edge," The Washington Post, May 2, 1987, p. G-1.

Elizabeth Venant, "Grand designs," Los Angeles Times Magazine, May 3, 1987, p. 13.

"The illusion of chaos: an interview with Frank O. Gehry, FAIA," Architecture California, September/October, 1987, p. 18.

1988

"The Loyola Forum–Frank Gehry," Places, A Quarterly Journal of Environmental Design, (MIT Press, Cambridge, MA, 1988), p. 42.

Daryl H. Miller, "Frank Gehry's architectural artistry," Los Angeles Daily News–L.A. Life, February 16, 1988, p. 15.

Lawrence Biemiller, "California campuses in the 80's: playfulness and human scale," The Chronicle of Higher Education, June 8, 1988, p. B-5.

Brooks Adams, "Frank Gehry's Merzbau," Art in America (New York, November, 1988), p. 144.

1989
Sam Hall Kaplan, "Architect Gehry Named Pritzker Prize Laureate," Los Angeles Times, May 1, 1989, VI-1.

Daryl H. Miller, "Architecture's top honor," Los Angeles Daily News–L.A. Life, May 1, 1989, p. 4.

Cathleen McGuigan, "A renegade takes the prize," Newsweek, May 22, 1989.

Hunter Drohojowska, "Frank Gehry's grand allusions, "Art News (New York, October, 1989), p. 116.

1990
"Best of the Decade," Time, January 1, 1990, p. 103.

Paul Goldberger, "Critic's notebook; Frank Gehry project to build a vision from the U.S. in Paris," The New York Times, May 15, 1990.

1991
Cathleen McGuigan, "A maverick master," Newsweek, June 17, 1991, p. 50.

1992
"Three architects share Wolf Prize for arts," The Jerusalem Post, January 16, 1992.

1993
Global Architecture, GA Architect 10: Frank O. Gehry (Tokyo 1993).

1998
Francesco Dal Co & Kurt W. Forster, Frank O. Gehry: The Complete Works (The Monacelli Press, New York 1998).

Jacob Weisberg, "Give that man another Guggenheim!" Slate (www.slate.com/id/9799, posted December 6, 1998).

1999
Joseph Rykwert, "An American original," Los Angeles Times Book Review, May 2, 1999, p. 6.

2000
Gerald T. McLaughlin, Loyola Law School: A Sense of Purpose and A Sense of Mission (Loyola Law School, Los Angeles, 2000).

2001
Frank Gehry, Architect (J. Fiona Ragheb, ed., Guggenheim Museum, New York 2001).

2002
Jason Miller & Susan Lauzau, Frank Gehry (Friedman, Michael Publishing, 2002).

2003
James Verini, "Frank Gehry's L.A.," Los Angeles Times Calendar/Weekend, September 11, 2003, p. 34.

2007
Lawrence B. Chollet, The Essential Frank O. Gehry (Harry N. Abrams, Inc., New York, 2007).

Laura Massino Smith, Tour of Frank Gehry Architecture & Other L.A. Buildings (Shiffer Publishing, Pennsylvania, 2007).

Pawel Szychalski, The Role of Gesture in Frank O. Gehry's Architecture (Licentiate thesis 2007, Department of Architecture and Built Environment, Lund University, Sweden).

2009
Barbara Isenberg, Conversations with Frank Gehry (Alfred A. Knopf, New York 2009).

Christopher Hawthorne, "At 80, Gehry sees his best-laid plans shift beneath him," Los Angeles Times, March 1, 2009, p. 1.

About the author   Robert Benson is Emeritus Professor of Law at Loyola Law School. He was a member of the committee that selected Frank Gehry as campus architect in 1979. Later, he and his wife asked Gehry to design a house for them, where they still live.